ACKNOWLEDGEMENTS

Dr Margaret Gibson, who supplied the photographs of medals.

This pamphlet has been edited by Iain Smith

The publication of a pamphlet by The Historical Association does not necessarily imply the Association's official approval of its contents.

Designed and prepared by Colin Barker

©Irene Collins, 1986

ISBN0 85278 288 8

Originated and published by The Historical Association, 59a Kennington Park Road, London SE11 4JH and printed in Great Britain by The Chameleon Press Limited, 5-25 Burr Road, Wandsworth, London SW18 4SG

The Historical Association, founded in 1906, brings together people who share an interest in, and love for, the past. It aims to further the study and teaching of history at all levels; teacher and student, amateur and professional. Membership offers a wide range of publications and journals at generous discounts and also gives access to courses, conferences, tours and branch activities. Full details are available from The Secretary, The Historical Association, 59a Kennington Park Road, London SE11 4JH, telephone: 01-735 3901.

Front cover and page 11: A sketch made during Napoleon's coronation ceremony by J.-L. David

Back cover: Part of a caricature by James Gillray, published in London, 1805. Napoleon and Josephine walk in their coronation procession, preceded by the Pope, for whom Napoleon's uncle, Cardinal Fesch, is swinging incense. They are attended by Napoleon's sisters. Napoleon's train is held by the subservient powers of Europe.

Contents

Over 100 medals were struck at the Paris Medal Mint, 1802-14, to commemorate the highlights of Napoleon's career.

(a) Medal struck to remind the French people of Napoleon's conquest of Egypt, 1798. Napoleon appears as a Roman general riding in triumph in a chariot drawn by two camels.

(b) The Concordat. Religion, who has been drooping over a discarded cross and bible, with a ruined church in the background, is helped to her feet by Prudence, holding out the mirror of Reflection, with Notre Dame in the background. Between them is the Gallic cock (vigilance) and the thunderbolt of Jupiter (Napoleon's armed power). The allegory implies that the Church, having learned by experience, will need to be more circumspect in the future.

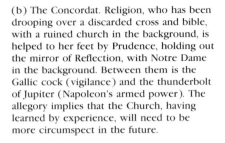

(c) Napoleon compares himself to Charlemagne, 1806.

The actual diameter of the medals is 40mm.

(d) Medal struck to celebrate Napoleon's victories at the start of the 1814 campaign for the defence of France. The Napoleonic eagle stands on a thunderbolt, with the star of destiny over its head.

Napoleon

First Consul and Emperor
of the French

Four years after the battle of Waterloo, Richard Whately[1] published a philosophical essay in which he argued that there was no real proof of Napoleon's existence. The deeds attributed to him were either so wondrously good or so amazingly bad that they far outran the evidence available to support them: Napoleon was a legendary figure with no more substance than Achilles.

*Since Whately expressed these **Historic Doubts concerning Napoleon Buonaparte** (1819), a great deal of evidence has been made available to historians. Vast numbers of reminiscences have been published, hundredweights of Napoleon's letters printed and official records of numerous governments opened up. Yet there is still a regrettable lack of information on some aspects of Napoleon's régime. Meanwhile more than 200,000 books and articles have been written on the subject, and historians continue to differ widely in their views. The object of this pamphlet is to point out the uncertainties of knowledge and the scope for differences of opinion on some important aspects of Napoleon's rule over the French people.*

Napoleon's rise to power

Thiers' *Histoire du Consulat et de l'Empire*,[2] published in the middle of the nineteenth century, began a tradition whereby France at the time of Napoleon's *coup d'état* was described as a country wracked by civil war, devastated by foreign invasion and disillusioned with parliamentary government. Roads were said to be impassable, canals unnavigable, ports desolate. Trade and industry were at a standstill. There was virtually no administration, no justice, no safety. To crown all, Britain had formed a Second Coalition whose armies were threatening France's frontiers whilst royalist revolt had broken out in Toulouse and Bordeaux. France was in imminent danger of a Bourbon restoration in which all the achievements of the Revolution would be lost. The French people, understandably, turned against the ineffective parliamentary régime of the Directory and welcomed the chance of strong government under a general who was renowned not only for his victories in Italy and Egypt but for his law making and his enlightened rule.

It has long been known that this gloomy picture of France in 1799 was derived from reports sent in to Napoleon by his newly appointed officials, all of whom had an interest in blackening the previous régime in order to justify the *coup d'état.* Their information is now treated with scepticism. No historian has pretended that all was well with France in 1799, but the efforts of the Directory to establish a sound financial and administrative system are better appreciated. Although dogged by a serious economic depression, the Directory is seen to have restored a measure of prosperity to France by 1799. Brigandage continued to cripple the western departments, but royalist revolt was put down in the south-west and the armies of the Directory won substantial victories over the Second Coalition in the Dutch Republic and Switzerland. France was in no need of a saviour. How, then, do we account for the rise of Napoleon?

The answer favoured by leading French historians emphasises the role of France's property owners, who are said to have been so shaken by the combined threat of a royalist rising and a foreign invasion that they could no longer trust the Directory in spite of its successes. In particular, they were afraid that a renewal of the crisis might bring Jacobins to power. The Directors had done their best to get rid of Jacobinism, but it remained strongly entrenched in parliament and in local administration. Napoleon's unexpected return from Egypt on 9 October 1799 offered the chance of strong government without the Jacobins, whose ideas were seen as a threat to property. Napoleon was the saviour not of France but of France's property-owning classes.

A slight confusion is introduced into this thesis by a tendency among French historians to refer to these classes as the bourgeoisie when it is well known that most of their members were landowners. As Alfred Cobban[3] pointed out some years ago, the term 'bourgeois' had a different meaning in eighteenth-century France, where it was used to denote any non-noble who was wealthy enough to live without working, from the one later given to it by Karl Marx. This is less of a problem, however, than the fact that there is no hard evidence as to what France's property-owners thought and wanted. Parliamentary elections might reasonably be expected to give some sort of a guide, since voting at the final stage was confined to property owners; but analyses of election results under the Directory have proved to be ambiguous. Only a third of the seats in the two legislative Councils were refilled each year, and in 1797 Royalists were successful and in 1798 Jacobins. In both cases the turn-out at the polls was extremely poor, and it can be argued that neither result indicated the views of the greater part of the electorate. It cannot be assumed, however, that the men who abstained from voting were disillusioned by the existing régime and ready to welcome Napoleon.

The strict Marxist interpretation of Napoleon's rise to power is that France's property-owners were propelled, whether they knew it or not, by the interests of the industrial and commercial bourgeoisie. Businessmen needed peace in order to expand their affairs, but they also needed to control foreign markets, and this inevitably meant war with Britain. The Directory could not be relied upon to win such a war: only Napoleon, the one general who had never been defeated, could promise peace on a basis of victory. Circumstantial evidence may be difficult to gather, but the thesis fits the pattern of universal history.

A different explanation has been put forward by Martyn Lyons.[4] The main problem for the Directory, he says, was the 'cloud of political apathy' which descended upon France after the hectic years of the Revolution. Under the Jacobins, men had been obliged to take part in politics, since indifference was a crime which might lead to the guillotine. Under the more liberal rule of the Directory they were glad to sink back into the obscurity of private life. Local officials were supposed to be elected in the cantons, but few men could be persuaded to accept posts: a veritable 'strike of administrators' prevented the Directory from taking a firm hold on the provinces. Political apathy also kept moderate republicans away from the polls and enabled extremist minorities to take advantage of the electoral system. The Directors could suitably have compromised with the extremists, who had abandoned illicit plots in favour of election by due process of law, but the Directors were afraid to adopt such a policy. Instead, they called on the army to expel Royalists from parliament in 1797, and persuaded the legislature to annul the return of Jacobins in 1798. These actions narrowed the government's basis of support and caused the electorate to become disenchanted with the electoral process. No one lifted a finger to protest when the Directory was destroyed by Napoleon's *coup d'état* in 1799. To many people the *coup* must simply have looked like another Directorial manoeuvre, replacing the panel of five Directors with a panel of three Consuls.

Political apathy is no more susceptible of proof than political disillusionment, but the refusal of the Directors to accept the consequences of the democratic process is plain to see. Three American historians, Lynn Hunt, David Lansky and Paul Hanson,[5] have carried the point further and argued that the Directors also refused to countenance the growth of political parties lest they should mobilise the masses. The labouring population had been given only a preliminary vote by the Constitution of 1795, but Royalists and Jacobins had already begun to appeal to a mass platform, and their efforts had brought considerable success at elections. The government had clamped down on their activities, but it could not expect repressive measures to succeed for long. Short of organising a political party of its own to appeal to the masses, and thereby alienating its moderate republican supporters, the government could do little else but seek a revision of the Constitution such as would eliminate political activity altogether. It was for this reason that one of the Directors, Siéyès, plotted with his friends to bring Napoleon to power.

This account focuses attention upon the instigators of the *coup d'état*. Unfortunately it assumes that they intended Napoleon to seize power, whereas Siéyès said afterwards that he had merely intended Napoleon to destroy the Directory, and then withdraw from the political scene. Siéyès' motives have never been fully elucidated, and the precise nature of the bargain he made with Napoleon is not known. He is usually credited with having wished to give France a perfect constitution of his own making, but he failed to produce a draft of such a constitution at the crucial moment, although his friends had long believed him to be carrying one around with him in his briefcase. When a committee met to draft a new constitution he provided a few notes as a basis for discussion, but his wishes with regard to the executive power remain obscure.

The committee which drew up the

Constitution of 1799 was chosen from among the members of the two Councils of the Directory. The machinations by which the conspirators won support on the Councils have been only partly uncovered, but money is known to have changed hands and it was probably not by coincidence that Napoleon's brother Lucien was elected President of the Council of Five Hundred. From this position he played a crucial role in securing the success of the *coup d'état* on 10 November 1799.

Public opinion

How popular was Napoleon once he had come to power? The plebiscites, taken in 1799 to confirm his position as First Consul for ten years, in 1802 to confirm his Life Consulship and in 1804 to make his title of Emperor hereditary, used to be regarded by historians as proof of widespread support for Napoleon. All Frenchmen over the age of 21 and in possession of civil rights were allowed to vote — an electorate estimated at the time at about five million. In 1799 the official results were said to be 3,011,007 for, and 1,562 against; in 1802, 3,600,000 for, and 8,374 against; and in 1804, 3,572,329 for, and 2,569 against. On all three occasions Napoleon had won a huge majority not only of the votes cast but of the potential electorate. Many people had abstained, but a 60 per cent poll was high for any vote taken in the early nineteenth century.

It has since been discovered, however, that the size of the affirmative vote was exaggerated. In 1799 Lucien Bonaparte, newly appointed as Minister of the Interior, falsified the results sent in from the departments in such a way as to more than double the number of affirmative votes. Moreover, demographers now estimate the electorate to have been nearly eight million, which means that the abstention rate was truly massive.

Fewer people voted for Napoleon than had voted for the Jacobin constitution in 1793. In the second plebiscite there was no tampering with the vote by the central authorities, but prefects in the departments sent in such results as they knew would please their superiors, sometimes recording unanimous support when in fact no poll had been taken. The same thing happened in 1804. A round figure of 450,000 yesses was also added for the army, although it had not been polled. It seems unlikely that the troops were so solidly in favour of the hereditary principle, when they had accounted for 40 per cent of the opposition votes in 1802.

Apart from the plebiscites, Napoleon blocked all channels along which public opinion normally expresses itself. Newspapers were reduced in number and censored in content; publishers and booksellers were obliged to apply for a limited number of licences which could be withdrawn at any time; the right of petition was drastically curtailed and public meetings could be held only with the permission of the police. The fact that these restrictions were imposed at all might be thought to indicate that serious opposition was known to exist; but it should be remembered that Napoleon was inherently suspicious of the press and of political organisations.

There was an electoral system, but it was designed for purposes other than that of reflecting the political views of the voters. The system adopted at the beginning of the Consulate was invented by Siéyès, and its main purpose was to produce vast lists of people who were thought fit to occupy official positions at communal, departmental and national levels (the last including membership of parliament). When this fantastic operation was mounted for the first time in 1801 there proved to be great competition to get on to the lists, even at the communal stage, because present and future employment was seen to be at stake. The authenticity of the lists was vigorously contested by unsuccessful candidates, and so much scorn was poured on the system that Napoleon abolished it in 1802 and devised another, which operated from 1803 until the end of the Empire. The main purpose of the new system was to designate groups of people who could be used as intermediaries between the government and the people (not *vice versa*). All adult males met in cantonal assemblies and elected life members to 'colleges' (or boards) representing the departments and their component arrondissements. Once every five years the colleges produced lists of parliamentary candidates (about ten for each available seat); and meanwhile they served as groups of 'notables' on whom Napoleon could bestow favours such as posts in local administration. The members of departmental colleges, unlike those of arrondissement colleges, had to be chosen from among the 600 biggest taxpayers in their department, and Napoleon showed a particular affection for them, believing that by addressing speeches to them and showering rewards on them he could demonstrate his regard for the propertied classes of the nation. Attendance at the meetings of colleges turned out to be poor, but this could have been due to the fact that no travelling expenses were paid and no board and lodging provided.

In the absence of other sources of information, prefects were expected to send in to the Minister of the Interior each month a report on public opinion in their department. These reports have never been systematically studied, although historians frequently dip into them. Their reliability is difficult to determine. Sometimes prefects seem to be writing from the heart, but in 1810 no less a person than the Minister of the Interior, Montalivet, said that the reports were useless — the prefects wrote whatever suited them best.

The nature of the régime

The Napoleonic régime in France is often referred to as a military dictatorship. As usual in times of war, the army was visible everywhere. All large towns had garrisons; troops were constantly seen marching along the roads; incidents involving damage to property and brutality to women were common. At no time, however, was the army called upon to interfere in politics as it had done under the Directory. Military glory had been a prerequisite of Napoleon's rise to power, and he believed that he would fall from power unless he continued to be victorious in war, but the predominance that he gave to the army was social rather than political. Of the 32,000 members of the Legion of Honour, created in 1802 to recognise civilian as well as military achievement, 97 per cent were military men. Of the 3,364 persons known to have been given titles in the imperial nobility created in 1808, 59 per cent were military. Of the 23 marshals, five became princes and the rest dukes. Military men also received the majority of the endowments created by Napoleon — grants of rent from lands in conquered countries, averaging five million francs a year, at a time when most workers received less than two francs a day.

Napoleonic France is also described as a police state. According to Louis Bergeron,[6] only the Habsburg monarchy had previously given the police so privileged a position. This judgment rests in part on Napoleon's liking for spies: Fouché, as Minister of Police, employed spies, as did Dubois, the prefect of police in Paris; but Napoleon had his own spies, and nothing pleased him better than to be able to cap the information provided by others. The Ministry of Police, suppressed in 1802, was revived in 1804, and when Fouché was replaced at the head of it by Savary in 1810 its proceedings became much more brutal. A decree of 1810 created political prisons and allowed suspects to be detained without trial on an order of the Privy Council. Jacques Godechot[7] has pointed out that only 2,500 persons were found to have been arbitrarily imprisoned when the Empire fell, but alongside this it should be noted that prefects could confine suspected dissidents to their houses whenever special security arrangements were required.

Napoleon's political ideas owed much to the Enlightenment, but he is sometimes thought to be precluded from qualifying as an Enlightened Despot by his repudiation of political philosophers with their generalised views of justice and human rights. Unlike Joseph II and Frederick the Great, who invited *philosophes* to their courts and studied their ideas, Napoleon went to considerable trouble to manoeuvre the *idéologues* out of the political arena. Benjamin Constant, Daunou, Guingené of the *Décade philosophique*, and several others who had supported the *coup d'état* in 1799 under the impression that Napoleon admired their ideas, were 'purged' from parliament in 1801. Their patroness, Madame de Staël, was exiled from Paris. The scholars whom Napoleon appointed to his ministries and his Council of State were experts in some particular branch of public affairs — law, finance, agriculture.

Most historians are in no doubt that Napoleon exercised a dictatorship. The Constitution of 1799, by which he was made First Consul for ten years, gave him not only complete control of the executive but a share of legislative power. Though bills had to be passed by a parliament, only Napoleon could initiate them and only he could amend them. No sooner did he encounter opposition from parliament than he began a double process of weakening its powers and exerting political control over it. The Tribunate, the only one of the two houses of parliament which had the right to discuss bills, was gradually depleted in size, and in 1807 abolished altogether. The second of the two houses, the Legislative Body, was then allowed to discuss bills as well as vote on them, but it was required to do most of its work in committees. Napoleon increased his influence over the membership, not by creating a political party and thereby giving in to the notion of parliamentary politics but by persuading the Senate, which chose the members of the Legislative Body from among the candidates submitted by the electoral colleges, to choose 'safe' men. The Senate was originally a somewhat obstreperous body, since half of its members were nominated by Siéyès; but Napoleon gradually packed it with supernumeraries, and allotted prizes in the form of huge estates in the provinces to those who proved most obsequious.

Within this framework it is possible to show that parliament was never wholly without significance. Napoleon believed that the proper functions of a parliament were to pass fundamental legislation and to receive the financial accounts of the government. Fundamental laws establishing new administrative, financial, judicial and educational systems were fairly numerous during the Consulate, but they became fewer as time went on: as one Councillor of State put it, 'Creation ends, life begins'. Sessions of parliament, which originally lasted four months, contracted to six weeks. Napoleon nevertheless continued to summon parliament annually to receive an account of how the government had spent the taxpayers' money, financial accountability having been regarded during the Enlightenment as the supreme sign of good government. As time went on, he was persuaded to present his financial demands to parliament in a single bill annually, thus laying the foundations for a genuine budgetary procedure. He was always irritated by opposition: in his view the duty of a parliament was to co-operate in the great work of legislation by accepting the government's measures and commending them to the public. In spite of his efforts, however, he never succeeded in getting rid of parliamentary opposition entirely: there was a sizable minority vote against the Code of Criminal Procedure in 1808, when Napoleon's prestige might have been thought to be at its height.

One historian, François Pietri,[8] has gone as far as to suggest that Napoleon always accepted parliamentary restraints, but there has been little or no support for this point of view. Frédéric Bluche,[9] the only historian to have attempted a history of Bonapartism, has argued more acceptably that Napoleon established a caesarian democracy, based on

plebiscites and buttressed by appeals to divine and hereditary sanctions. By virtue of the first plebiscite, Napoleon could claim to have become sole representative of the people. By virtue of the second, he could claim that the people had bestowed absolute power on him for an indefinite period. By the third they could be said to have extended this power to his heirs. Napoleon was not content with receiving delegated power, however: he was determined to show that sovereignty no longer belonged to the nation but had been transferred from the people to his dynasty for ever. He fulfilled his purpose in the ritual of the coronation at Notre Dame. When he had been consecrated by the Pope, he took the crown from the altar, raised it high above the congregation, and himself placed it on his head. As depicted in a sketch by David it was an arrogant gesture, but it was not unpremeditated. It had been arranged beforehand with the Pope, who also agreed to consecrate Napoleon as a sign that he had been found worthy by God. Napoleon henceforward styled himself 'Napoleon, by the grace of God and the Constitution, Emperor of the French', a formula which echoed the mystical union supposed to have taken place between king and nation in former coronation ceremonies at Reims. He seems to have found difficulty in maintaining the metaphors of divine and hereditary sovereignty, however; he still, on occasion, referred to a 'contract' having been formed between himself and the nation, and it was this theory which surfaced among the Senators after his defeat by the Allies in 1814, providing them with an excuse to declare that he had forfeited the crown.

Modern dictators make much use of propaganda, and Napoleon can be shown to have been adept at the art. He is without doubt one of the most theatrical figures ever to have ruled a country; every step he took was calculated for its effect on the gallery. No opportunity was neglected. He wrote articles for newspapers and composed a new catechism for the church. He held lavish displays, such as the annual state opening of parliament, and presented new standards, surmounted by eagles, to army regiments encamped at Boulogne. He paid carefully devised visits to people who had been kind to him in his youth, and provided dowries for 4,500 young ladies who agreed to marry disabled soliders on the day of his own wedding to Marie-Louise. He founded museums and patronised the arts. By no means all the publicity given to his exploits was contrived, however. Many artists spontaneously painted pictures exalting his image. Sculptors and medal engravers vied with each other to represent him as a Roman warrior or a Greek hero, and it was not an imperial decree but the mysterious dictates of fashion which promoted the ubiquitous Empire style of dress, furniture and interior design.

Legislation

Napoleon's classical education, reinforced by the Enlightenment, taught him that the supreme duty of a ruler was to make laws. From the outset he took his legislative duties very seriously, the more so since they were connected with the maintenance of law and order, which he regarded as the essence of his régime. He was as proud of his legislative achievements as of his victories in war: when David painted a portrait of him in his study, with a parchment in the desk displaying the word 'Code' and a map of Austerlitz half unrolled on the carpet, a candle guttering to its end and the hands of the clock standing at 4.13, he exclaimed delightedly, 'You have found me out, my dear David! At night I work for my subjects' happiness and by day I work for their glory'.

In discussing his major pieces of

legislation — the local government act, the organisation of the judiciary, the education act, the establishment of the Bank of France, the Civil Code — historians readily assume that Napoleon was personally responsible for the more authoritarian aspects of each measure. Thus he is frequently credited with the idea of appointing a prefect to head the administration in each department, of having judges nominated by the state instead of elected by the people, of establishing state control over education, of allowing only the Bank of France to issue notes, and of increasing the legal authority of parents over children and husbands over wives. He undoubtedly created the climate in which such proposals could be produced, but his own contribution to the origin of any particular law is difficult to determine. His ministers individually approached him, or were summoned by him, to discuss the need for specific measures. They then communicated with the Council of State, which was divided into sections for drafting bills. All drafts were discussed in full Council before being presented to parliament, and Napoleon took care to be present when important items were on the agenda, but only the most formal minutes were taken. History is therefore dependent on subsequent memoirs and chance revelations for knowledge of what went on. The only measure which can be said for certain to have come from Napoleon's personal initiative is the establishment of the Legion of Honour, to which the majority of the members of the Council of State were opposed. Napoleon presided over 55 of the 107 sessions devoted to discussion of the Civil Code (later called the Code Napoléon), but the only issue on which he is known to have intervened decisively is that of divorce by mutual consent on grounds of incompatibility. Jean Tulard has concluded that Napoleon's chief contribution to the work of legislation was to speed up

completion of measures which the Revolutionaries had contemplated for years; but to reduce Napoleon's status to that of a timetable would hardly account for the immense reputation he enjoyed in his own day. Though he clearly owed much to his ministers and Councillors of State, whom he had himself appointed, it would seem equally inappropriate to turn him into a committee.

No one has ever denied Napoleon's individual responsibility for the Concordat, which originated as a treaty between France and the Holy See; but the importance attributed to it may have to be modified in view of Olwen Hufton's[10] researches into the revival of Catholic worship during the period of the Directory. These show that, thanks to the spontaneous efforts of ordinary men and women (especially women) in the parishes, many churches had been re-opened and priests persuaded to officiate. This movement had apparently gone so far that any ruler would have been foolish not to take it on board. Nevertheless, Republican politicians were antagonistic to government recognition of the church, and those clergy who in 1790 had sworn allegiance to the Revolution (including the formidable Abbé Grégoire) were opposed to negotiations with the Pope. Napoleon's intervention prevailed over these obstacles, and although the rivalry between former 'constitutional' and 'refractory' clergy made the Concordat difficult to establish in some parts of the country, schism eventually died down.

The question usually asked about Napoleon's legislation is the extent to which it fulfilled the aims of the Revolution. The answer depends on what may be understood as the aims of the Revolution. In 1789 a wide area of individual freedom was envisaged, and the electoral principle was applied to parliament, local assemblies, local officials, judges and justices of the peace. In 1793, both achievements were suspended in the interests of safeguarding the Republic, and not until the Directory came to power did France return more or less to the situation that had obtained in 1789. Napoleon encroached upon individual liberty with his press censorship and his police measures, and he removed the electoral principle from all positions except those of members of parliament and justices of the peace. By contrast he maintained the two great Revolutionary achievements of abolishing feudalism and establishing equality before the law.

The administrative system also saw changes. In 1789, hostility to the Bourbon state resulted in the abolition of the system of *intendants,* and central control over the localities was thereby rendered impossible. The Jacobins, faced with rebellion in a number of local centres and anxious to mobilise the population for war, tried to remedy the situation by appointing *représentants en mission* to the provinces. The Directory moved a step further towards centralisation by appointing *commissaires* to the departments. Napoleon replaced them by prefects, the main difference being that the last no longer had to be chosen from among the inhabitants of the department they administered. The extent to which they succeeded in centralising the administration remains questionable. Tocqueville[11] made a classic judgment when he described the prefects as '*intendants* writ large', but although the Revolution had removed the privileged corporations which hampered the *intendants,* the influence of local notables remained strong for the rest of the nineteenth century, and a prefect who wished to be successful had to win their co-operation.

Education is another debatable area. The Revolutionaries of 1789 paid no attention to it in spite of their insistence on 'the career open to talent'. The Jacobins declared their intention of providing free, compulsory and secular education at the primary level, but in fact they had neither time nor money for founding new schools. Meanwhile existing schools, almost all of which were run by clergy, closed down when the church was persecuted. The Directory concentrated on secondary education, setting up a number of 'central schools'; entrance was by fees, but a policy of awarding scholarships was under discussion. Napoleon made no promises about primary education — his spokesman told parliament that the state had no right to spend money unrelated to its needs; but the Concordat enabled the church to re-open its schools, and Napoleon promptly had a medal struck in honour of 'Education Restored'. Secondary education was declared to be a proper concern of the state, because civil servants and army officers might be recruited from secondary schools; but concern revealed itself as much in a determination to control syllabuses as to provide places. The central schools were closed down and replaced by 34 *lycées,* still fee-paying but with 6,000 scholarships offered by the state — an invidious provision when half the communes in France had no primary schools. The syllabus was designed not, as one might have expected, to promote the study of technical or even scientific subjects but to restore the emphasis on the classics, which the Directory, in its central schools, had sought to modify.

In the Tribunate a solitary opponent of Napoleon's educational policies described them as élitist. The Legion of Honour was more widely criticised as a departure from the revolutionary principle of equality, even though Napoleon abandoned the stipends which he had intended to attach to the awards. The creation of an imperial nobility six years later could be considered an even greater departure, although the titles carried no legal privileges or tax immunities. Napoleon claimed that by establishing a nobility based on service to the state, rather than on birth, he had finally destroyed the old aristocracy and safeguarded equality; but the force of the argument was somewhat lessened by the provision that titled persons with sufficient wealth to create an entail could apply to have their titles made hereditary.

Social classes

The nature of French society in Napoleonic times has been under scrutiny from French scholars for more than a decade, with British and American historians for the most part standing on the sidelines. Statistical and computerised methods have been brought to bear on the old textbook cliché that Napoleon reconciled the aristocracy of the ancien régime with the bourgeoisie of the Revolution and produced a new governing élite, to which men of humble origin could also be promoted. Different definitions of the governing élite have been employed. Jean Tulard,[12] for instance, has studied the social composition of the imperial nobility. Of the 3,364 men whom he has been able to identify as having received titles, he has discovered that rather more than 20 per cent came from the former nobility, nearly 60 per cent from the bourgeoisie and nearly 20 per cent from the popular classes. This bears out the textbook assertion.

Two other historians, Louis Bergeron and Guy Chaussinand-Nogaret,[13] have studied the members of all the arrondissement and departmental colleges in 1810, feeding into a computer the details of as many as 7,000 men. The results of their study are obscure, but Geoffrey Ellis,[14] who has complemented it by taking soundings in the statistics of two contrasting areas of France, considers that it gives a different picture from that provided by Tulard's imperial nobility. A far lower percentage were pre-Revolution nobles: perhaps, after all, the majority of former aristocrats was unwilling to serve in politics. A higher proportion were businessmen — 11 per cent as compared with one per cent for the imperial nobility; suggesting that businessmen were better thought of in the provinces, where they were active in chambers of commerce, than by Napoleon. A very high proportion were bureaucrats: in this respect there was continuity from pre-Revolution days, when office-holders enjoyed great prestige in the countryside. Unfortunately no clue is given as to how many of the local notables were men of humble birth, since the lists show only their wealth and current occupation.

Bergeron and Chaussinand-Nogaret[15] are now directing a team of scholars engaged in producing alphabetical lists, department by department, of yet another group — the lists of 60 to 90 persons whom each prefect, at the request of Napoleon, designated as the most distinguished notables in his department. These studies have so far covered only half the country, but the pattern which seems to be emerging is similar to that of Tulard's imperial nobility, except that men of humble birth, who owed their titles mainly to military service, are usually absent from the civilian scene. This brings us back to where we started. Studies of prefects and of members of parliament give much the same results, always remembering that things were rather different at the very beginning of the Consulate when there were more former Revolutionaries around.

The study of social classes in Napoleonic France has long suffered from a serious imbalance of source material. Historians have preferred to study the élites, for which some well-defined sources are available, rather than the poorer classes, on which information can only be obtained from a multiplicity of prefects' reports and local records. From the few local studies that have been published, it appears that the number of peasant proprietors continued to expand, as the last of the national land came on to the market and as impoverished nobles sold off part of their estates; but the majority could buy only very small plots of land, insufficient to supply their own needs. The quality of the land was for the most part poor. The myth that Napoleon was the friend of humble peasants is one of the strangest facets of the Napoleonic Legend, since it is hard to see that he did anything for them except conscript their sons and requisition their mules and carts for war.

On the lower classes in the towns, ignorance is such that historians contradict each other as to whether there was a shortage of labour, caused by the war, or a superfluity of labour, caused by demographic pressure on the land and by deserters from the army taking shelter in the towns. However bad conditions may have been, workers had little chance of protesting, as the ban imposed in 1791 on workers' coalitions was reiterated in 1803 and workers were not adequately represented on arbitration boards. The government possessed a potentially powerful weapon in the *livret* or job record, but there is little information on how it was used.

Statistics show that it was fairly easy for artisans and shop assistants to climb into the lower middle class by renting or purchasing a small property and setting up in business on their own. In provincial towns they sometimes did well, but in Paris there was little chance of them rising any higher in the business world, which was more and more confined to established families. In the professions it was equally hard

to rise into the top grades. Napoleon created vast numbers of low paid jobs in the civil service, but the better paid ones went either to men who had had some administrative experience already or to connections of the Bonaparte family. Even in the army, new recruits might become lieutenants but none found a marshal's baton in his knapsack. In this respect, society was less open than it had been during the Revolution. The question arises as to how much the French people had gained from the Revolutionary principle of the career open to talent, which Napoleon so much prided himself on carrying out. Recent research has shown that comparatively few families, which first rose to prominence in banking, administration or the army, subsequently put out tentacles in all these concerns, and by judicious marriages and careful investment built up huge networks of influence and clientage. Such were the Berthiers, the Leclercs, the Périers, the Clarys, the Says and a number of other families whose grip on all spheres of importance, from the court to the stock exchange, made the Napoleonic Empire not altogether different from the ancien régime.

The economy

In the economic sphere, discussion ranges between the possibility that France under Napoleon reached the 'take-off' point in an industrial revolution and the view that the economy, though theoretically given unlimited opportunity for expansion by the abolition of feudalism, in fact completely stagnated. The former argument rests mainly on spectacular developments in the cotton and chemical industries. Both had made progress during the early part of the eighteenth century but had suffered during the Revolution. Recovery began under the Directory, but it was the psychological effect of greater stability under the Consulate and the opportunity to catch up with British technological advances during the Peace of Amiens that facilitated a break-through. From 1803 the cotton industry was decisively modernised in and around Paris, Rouen, Lille, Amiens and Mulhouse. The most important innovation was the increasing use of Britain's mule-jenny, which could spin both coarse and fine yarns and required little skill to operate (the French Jacquard loom for weaving was more complicated and made its biggest impact on high quality goods). Napoleon's ban on the importation of cotton cloth from India favoured spinning and weaving at the expense of calico printers, who had considered themselves to be something of an élite during the eighteenth century, but this imbalance was to some extent remedied by vertical development, with single firms controlling all processes. Closely connected with textiles, the chemical industry made crucial advances in the use of artificial instead of natural products. In this field, scientists rather than technicians played an important role in industry for the first time.

Some historians include the expansion of metallurgy as one of the high-spots of the period, but others exclude it on the grounds that more wood than coal was used for smelting, and more encouragement was given to afforestation than to exploitation of France's coal deposits. This obviously had a deleterious effect on the whole future of French industry. Technical progress was more or less confined to the two major industries, which became 'islands of modernity in the sea of traditional, *ancien-régime* type economy' (François Crouzet[16]). Though Paris became a great commercial and banking centre, facilities for credit remained insufficient to supply industrial need. Frenchmen continued to invest money in land rather than industry. In the hinterland of big Atlantic ports the development of new industries as an alternative to sea-borne commerce barely kept pace with 'de-industrialisation' as bigger areas were given over to pasture and to viticulture. Industrialisation, and the wealth that went with it, was confined to a few areas of the country, notably the north east and the Rhineland departments.

Above all, there was no agricultural revolution to sustain a future growth of industry. Wealthy men bought land for prestige purposes rather than for exploitation: they let out large areas in small lots to peasants, who continued with their traditional practices. High rents encouraged landlords to grant only short-term leases, and these in turn discouraged any outlay on agricultural inprovement. Little change took place in rural mentalities. Areas which had good natural pasture land intensified their cattle raising to supply nearby cities with meat, but other areas took no initiative in creating artificial meadows. Peasants grew a few potatoes to feed a pig, but potatoes as a diet were connected in the rural mind with poverty, and no great expansion of potato cultivation took place.

The relative prosperity enjoyed by France from 1803 to 1810 was shattered by a prolonged crisis during the next two or three years. This differed from all previous economic crises in that it was not caused initially by shortage of food; and although bad harvests in 1811 intensified panic, at no time did people die of starvation. The crisis resulted from a financial crash, caused by over-speculation in smuggled goods. Industry was adversely affected, employees were laid off and wages declined as food prices rose. In some places there was a shortage of manufactured goods. Some historians have seen the crisis as forming a watershed in the history of the régime, for though the government succeeded in supplying food to the towns, and severe repression soon restored order, the basic problems of low purchasing power and lack of credit had not been tackled and perhaps not even recognised. Crime remained endemic in the countryside, and inland from the eastern frontier the populace showed little enthusiasm for repelling foreign invaders in 1814.

Expansion and war

Napoleon's foreign policy has aroused more controversy than any other aspect of his career. For the historian concerned with Napoleon's performance as ruler of France, the leading question must be not his motives, which have been endlessly discussed, but the extent to which his policy was beneficial or detrimental to France. Between 1802 and 1812 Napoleon reshaped many of the boundaries of Europe and gave to both Italy and Germany a greater degree of unity than they had hitherto known. This is often counted to his credit as a statesman, but though it may in the short term have benefited France, who extended her influence over west Germany and north Italy, it came to be regarded as detrimental later in the nineteenth century when both powers escaped from France's orbit.

By the treaties of Lunéville (1801) and Amiens (1802) Napoleon secured recognition by Austria and Britain of France's natural frontiers (the Rhine, the Alps and the Pyrenees) for which she had fought since 1792. The acquisition of the Austrian Netherlands and of territories on the left bank of the Rhine was greatly to France's benefit since both areas, when fully released from feudalism and provided with wider markets, 'took off' into an industrial revolution and became economically the most advanced areas of the French Empire. Most of the inhabitants did not speak French, but neither did many people in, say, Brittany and Languedoc. The

imposition of French as the language of administration throughout the Empire has been seen by some historians as a significant aspect of bourgeois control.

Apart from Piedmont, Napoleon annexed no further territory until 1809-10 when military strategy took precedence over all other considerations. Prior to that time, he preferred to create beyond the natural frontiers a semi-circle of satellite states, covering the Dutch Republic, the Confederation of the Rhine, the Swiss cantons, Italy and Spain. Some of the satellite states were ruled by members of his own family and others by princes and monarchs who owed much to his patronage. Historians who believe that Napoleon's policy all along was to annex the satellite states to the French Empire forget that by doing so he would lose the chance to treat them as colonies. All were united to France by treaties which not only bound them to supply money and troops for Napoleon's wars but also to accept the Continental System, banning imports from Britain and her colonies and agreeing to admit French goods with reduced tariffs. They were also expected to supply raw materials for France's industries in preference to their own.

Recent work on the Continental System has concentrated on its role in the French economy rather than on its use as a weapon of war against Britain. According to Jean Meyer,[17] France had already, during the Revolution, abandoned the Bourbon policy of rivalling Britain in trans-Atlantic trade and had sacrificed the naval power which such a policy necessitated by using ships simply to support armies. The emphasis on armies rather than navies predicated a policy of commercial expansion on the continent. There Britain played into Napoleon's hands by virtually banning neutral ships from trading with French-controlled Europe. France exploited the continental markets that were thus opened up to her with considerable success until Napoleon's financial exactions drained the satellite states of purchasing power. The effect of the Continental System on the French economy is now seen to have been one of change rather than overall misery. Seaports were ruined, but inland distribution centres flourished. Cotton, which had been in direct competition with Britain, gained over silk. Contraband made as much money as Atlantic commerce had previously done, but it went through different hands.

France's expanding power and influence on the continent was both a cause and a result of war, which was waged against Britain continuously from 1803 to 1814 and against Austria, Prussia and Russia intermittently. There has been much discussion as to whether Britain, for strategic and economic reasons, could ever have been reconciled to France's acquisition of the Austrian Netherlands. The Continental System was certainly anathema to her, since she had previously exported a third of her manufactured goods to Europe. Russia was Britain's natural ally, since she relied on British ships to export her vast supplies of timber and naval stores; nevertheless, she allied with France from 1807 until she was invaded by Napoleon's Grand Army in 1812. Austria and Prussia lost territory as a result of France's acquisition of the natural frontiers, but each allied with France at one time or another and it is arguable that they could have been persuaded to accept French expansion in western Europe if France had helped them to spread their wings elsewhere. In the end, like Russia, they were antagonised by Napoleon's unfocused policies in eastern Europe and the Ottoman Empire. In 1814 France fought alone against invasion over her eastern frontier by Austria, Prussia and Russia whilst Britain occupied her south-western departments.

Napoleon is considered by D.G. Chandler[18] to have been one of the world's four greatest military commanders, yet he can be given no credit for the size and excellence of the armies that he led. The French people had first been mobilised for war by the Jacobins, and a means of combining enthusiasm with training had been devised by Carnot. The conscription law which Napoleon operated was passed by the Directory a year before he came to power. He introduced no new weapons, and his tactics were basically those invented during the Revolution. He came to rely more and more, however, on hurling vast numbers of troops at the enemy. His victories against Austria in 1809 cost him more casualties than he inflicted on his opponent. At this rate, as Michael Glover[19] has pointed out, even victory would eventually be self-defeating. France's population was increasing, but not as fast as it had increased in the eighteenth century: other nations were catching up.

Napoleon's reputation as a military leader rests entirely on his strategy and the degree to which he inspired his men. The brilliance of the former is debated by military historians, among whom the campaigns of 1805 leading to victory at Ulm and Austerlitz and of 1814 for the defence of France seem to be the only ones that are generally admired. In 1812, Napoleon's celebrated speed at moving armies across Europe proved a disadvantage in Russia, where the army outstripped the baggage trains he had decided to employ. His charismatic hold over his men has never been denied, although it is known that he did not treat them very well. He cut down the medical services that had been improved during the Revolution, and in fast-moving campaigns the sick and wounded were frequently left at the mercy of the enemy.

Napoleon often congratulated himself on fighting wars without increasing taxation. Not until 1813 did he attempt to raise the level of the three direct taxes bequeathed to him by the Revolution. On the other hand, from 1802 he reintroduced consumer taxes, which had been condemned in 1789 as unjust to the poor. He confined them to salt, tobacco and liquor, and for many years they were not heavy, since he could get most of the money he needed by imposing customs duties and by exacting heavy indemnities from the countries he conquered. From 1809 the Spanish War cost money which could not be recouped, but it was not until the collapse of French hegemony in Europe in 1813 that the whole burden of war fell on the French taxpayer. The indirect taxes then quadrupled in amount from when they were first levied.

No more than seven per cent of the total French population was required to go to the wars. Figures for loss of life seem now to have been agreed upon by demographers at 916,000 Frenchmen killed or missing without trace, the biggest proportion of the losses occurring in the last few years of the Empire. By twentieth-century standards this is a small number for a major combatant over 11 years of fighting. As a fraction of the French population it is not large; it scarcely equals the number that died in any one year from natural causes. Still, they were mostly young men who might otherwise have lived, married and produced children. An additional 114,500 men were invalided out of the army with severe wounds, often disabled for life. Their pensions cost more than the upkeep of the army in the field, although they were pitifully small (smaller for members of the rank and file than for officers, and smaller than those granted during the Revolution).

If the cost of the wars is seen in terms of human suffering, the question inevitably arises as to how far Napoleon was responsible for them. He was by training and temperament a soldier, and most historians agree that he turned very rapidly to military solutions. He himself continually said that he wanted peace and that war was forced on him by his enemies. A few historians have believed him. It is perfectly possible to argue, upon evidence, that Britain was responsible for breaking the Peace of Amiens in 1803 and that from this all else followed. Austria, Prussia and Russia were paid by Britain to put armies in the field in 1805-7. Spanish guerrilla resistance would have been nothing without the British expeditionary force. Austria was already rearming herself against France when Napeolon carried out his lightning campaign in 1809. In 1812 Napoleon invaded Russia because he believed that Tsar Alexander was preparing to ally with Britain, and there is every reason to suppose that Napoleon was right.

Marxist historians assert that war between France and Britain was the inevitable consequence of economic rivalry between the bourgeoisies of the two nations. This reduces Napoleon's responsibility to that of a mere agent of history. Jean Tulard[20] has varied the Marxist viewpoint by assigning the key role not to the bourgeoisie but to the notables (by which he means men who had made or retained wealth in one form or another during the Revolution). The notables raised Napoleon to the position of dictator and supported him in war against counter-revolutionary powers in order to safeguard their possessions. They began to have their doubts about him in 1808 when he invaded Spain, a move which seemed to them to have nothing to do with their interests. Their doubts were confirmed when the unexpected resistance of the Spanish people gave Britain a chance to break the stranglehold of the Continental

System. They began to regard Napoleon's régime no longer as authoritarian but as tyrannical, and to seek to impose controls upon it. After his defeats in Russia and Germany, their hitherto docile parliament asked for reform; and when Napoleon rejected their plea they negotiated for the return of the Bourbons. This argument may well be correct, but it needs a good deal of substantiating, and not everyone will agree with so deterministic a view.

Napoleon like Rousseau (whose writings he imitated in his youth) was full of contradictions. Whilst saying that he wanted peace he extolled the virtues of war. In classical times, military renown was allied to good government: Napoleon made the same equation when he presented to parliament the flags taken from the enemy. It was particularly appropriate, he said, that the Spanish Campaign should have opened at the same time as the parliamentary session. In his carefully prepared army bulletins he tried to persuade the whole population to share the sense of honour which led many soldiers to die rather than see their regimental standard captured by the enemy. Napoleon extolled war not because it might bring power or wealth to France but because it brought glory on the battlefield.

Not everybody was impressed. Draft-dodging and desertion, either from the conscription centres or on the march, was a continuous feature of the times and has been used by some historians as an index not only to the unpopularity of the wars but to the unpopularity of the whole régime. The figures are difficult to interpret. The proportion of deserters to conscripts actually fell from 27 per cent during the Consulate to 13 per cent during the wars of 1805-7 and 10 per cent in 1813, but the fall could have been due to the tightening up of controls and to severe penalties imposed on deserters who were caught. In any case, 10 per cent of conscripts in 1813 was a far bigger number than 27 per cent in 1800, because more men were called up. The desertion rate differed from one part of the country to another. It was low in the north as a result, it has been suggested, of high morale in the thriving industrial towns; high in the south, especially when conscripts knew they would be sent to the cruel Spanish War; low in the annexed Netherland departments and high in those of the former Piedmont; high in areas of forest and woodland which afforded shelter; higher in the countryside than the towns, possibly because young peasant conscripts who had lived all their life within the sound of the village church bell were bewildered by a visit to the recruiting town. Villagers often sheltered their own draft-dodgers but were hostile to bands of deserters from other regions.

There were other means of avoiding army service that are more difficult to assess than desertion. One was to get married. In 1813 the Minister of the Interior suggested, not altogether jokingly, that conscription had benefited France by encouraging marriages and thereby increasing the population. Moreover, throughout the period, conscripts were allowed to buy substitutes. After 1809 this did not safeguard them from being called up again a year or two later; but even so the prices paid for substitutes rose enormously. Even in 1812 there were men who were willing to go to the war in return for ready cash.

The Hundred Days

The First Treaty of Paris, imposed on France in May 1814 by the victorious Allies, is usually considered by historians to have been generous. Indeed, Napoleon himself regarded it so, although it exiled him to the island of Elba. However, when he escaped less than a year later, the mistakes made by the restored Bourbon king had already created a favourable atmosphere for him to re-establish his rule over France. The Allies, who were serious in their belief that he constituted a menace to European peace, had to defeat him all over again and exile him to the more distant St Helena. The terms imposed on France by the Second Treaty of Paris were understandably much harsher than those of 1814, but in spite of this ruinous outcome of Napoleon's adventure, his name was connected with the idea of patriotism in the minds of many Frenchmen for decades after. The Bourbons, along with the aristocracy and clergy who came in their wake, were widely regarded as alien: as David Pinkney[21] has shown, the Paris crowd which rebelled against Charles X in 1830 was not republican but Bonapartist.

During the Hundred Days, Napoleon had not appealed to popular sentiment so much as to the liberal elements which had begun to appear in the last years of the Empire. He established complete freedom of speech and a bicameral parliament with an elected lower chamber. The franchise, though based on the old electoral colleges, was wider than that granted by the Bourbon Charter of 1814. Yet when the new constitutional measure was put to the popular vote, only 2.15 per cent of the electorate went to the polls. On the grounds that the 1,554,112 men (99.6 per cent of the poll) who voted in the affirmative must have been the hard core of Napoleon's supporters, it has been suggested that the north-east and eastern regions of France, where most of them were to be found, constituted the real *foyers* of Bonapartism. This may or may not have been the case. These areas were the ones that had suffered most from the invasion of 1814. They were also the ones that had benefited most from industrialisation during the Empire. Yet the majority of the affirmative votes came from peasants.

The question as to whether Napoleon would have stuck to parliamentary rule had he been victorious at Waterloo is less important than the fact that he had woven another strand into the tangle of Bonapartist theory. By describing the bicameral parliament of the Hundred Days as a logical development of the Legislative Body and Senate, and by insisting that the constitution of 1815 was merely an 'additional act' to the constitutions of the Empire, he enabled his supporters to claim thereafter that the natural outcome of an authoritarian Bonapartist state was a Liberal Empire. The Hundred Days, which might have been a mere epilogue, became the prelude to a new era.

Notes

(Numbers in brackets refer to fuller references in the Select Reading List)

[1] R. Whately, *Historic Doubts concerning Napoleon Buonaparte* (first published 1819, new edition 1986).

[2] A. Thiers, *Histoire du Consulat et de l'Empire* (20 vols, 1845-62).

[3] A. Cobban, *The Social Interpretation of the French Revolution* (1964).

[4] M. Lyons (16)

[5] L. Hunt, D. Lansky and P. Hanson, 'The failure of the Liberal Republic in France, 1795-99', *Journal of Modern History*, 1979.

[6] L. Bergeron (3)

[7] J. Godechot, *Les Institutions de la France sous la Révolution et l'Empire* (2 vols, 1951).

[8] F. Pietri, *Napoléon et le Parlement, ou le dictature enchaîné* (1955).

[9] F. Bluche, *Le Bonapartisme* (Series "Que sais-je?", 1981).

[10] O. Hufton (15)

[11] A. de Tocqueville, *L'ancien régime et la Révolution* (1855).

[12] J. Tulard, *Napoléon et la noblesse de l'Empire* (1979).

[13] L. Bergeron et G. Chaussinand-Nogaret, *Les 'masses de granit': cent mille notables du premier empire* (1979).

[14] G. Ellis (15)

[15] L. Bergeron et G. Chaussinand-Nogaret, *Les Grandes notables du premier empire* (1978).

[16] F. Crouzet, 'French economic growth in the nineteenth century reconsidered', *History*, 1974.

[17] J. Meyer, 'L'Europe et la mer de 1778 à 1802' in *L'Europe à la fin du XVIIIe siècle* (1985).

[18] D.G. Chandler (4)

[19] M. Glover (11)

[20] J. Tulard (20)

[21] D.H. Pinkney, *The French Revolution of 1830* (Princeton, 1972).

Select list of further reading in English

(The place of publication is London, unless otherwise stated)

(1) E.E. Arnold, *Fouché, Napoleon and the General Police* (New York, 1979)
(2) C. Barnett, *Bonaparte* (1978), a hostile biography.
(3) L. Bergeron, *France under Napoleon* (Princeton, 1982), translated from the French edition of 1972. Particularly good on social and economic affairs.
(4) D.G. Chandler, *Napoleon* (1973), a good general survey by an expert in military history; chapter six summarises his magisterial work, *The Campaigns of Napoleon* (1966).
(5) C.H. Church, 'In search of the Directory' in J.F. Bosher (ed), *French Government and Society, 1500-1850* (1973).
(6) I. Collins, *Napoleon and his Parliaments* (1979).
(7) O. Connelly et al, *Historical Dictionary of Napoleonic France* (1985), short biographies, accounts of battles, etc.
(8) V. Cronin, *Napoleon* (1971), a biography which takes a very favourable view of Napoleon.
(9) F. Crouzet, 'Wars, blockade and economic change in Europe, 1792-1815', *Journal of Economic History*, 1964.
(10) G. Ellis, *Napoleon's Continental Blockade: the case of Alsace* (Oxford, 1981), looks at the 'land' rather than the 'sea' aspects of the Blockade.
(11) M. Glover, *The Napoleonic Wars: an illustrated history, 1792-1815* (1979), an excellent account of the armies and navies of all the major powers, as well as of the battles.
(12) D.J. Goodspeed, *Bayonets at St Cloud* (1965), a narrative account of the *coup d'état* of 1799.
(13) R.E. Holtman, *Napoleonic Propaganda* (Louisiana, 1950), the only full account of this subject.
(14) C. Jones, 'The Welfare of the French foot-soldier', *History*, 1980, covers the subject from the sixteenth century to Napoleon.
(15) G. Lewis and C. Lucas (eds), *Beyond the Terror* (Cambridge, 1983); see especially chapters by G. Ellis, 'Rhine and Loire: Napoleonic élites and social order', A. Forrest, 'Conscription and crime in rural France during the Directory and Consulate', and O. Hufton, 'The reconstruction of a church, 1796-1801'.
(16) M. Lyons, *France under the Directory* (Cambridge, 1975), the best account available in English.
(17) J.J. Mathews, 'Napoleon's military bulletins', *Journal of Modern History*, 1950, describes the use of bulletins as propaganda.
(18) A. Palmer, *An Encyclopaedia of Napoleon's Europe* (1984), similar to (7) but shorter and covers the whole of Europe.
(19) D.M.G. Sutherland, *France 1789-1815: Revolution and counter-revolution* (1968), stresses developments in the localities and questions the extent of centralisation.
(20) J. Tulard, *Napoleon: the myth of the saviour* (1984, translated from the French edition of 1977), synthesises much scholarly work; concludes with a lengthy, annotated bibliography.
(21) E.A. Whitcombe, *Napoleon's Diplomatic Service* (Durham, North Carolina, 1979), one of the few books on French administrative history.
(22) E.A. Whitcombe, 'Napoleonic Prefects', *American Historical Review*, 1974, analyses social background, training, length of service etc.
(23) I. Woloch, *The French Veteran: from the Revolution to the Restoration* (Chapel Hill, 1979), a fascinating account of the men invalided out of the army.
(24) D.G. Wright, *Napoleon and Europe* (Seminar Studies in History, 1984), a balanced account, short, with a few documents; suggests that views of Napoleon are largely a matter of temperament.

Extracts in English from Napoleon's Letters

(25) C. Herold, *The Mind of Napoleon* (1955).
(26) J.E. Howard, *Letters and Documents of Napoleon, 1769-1802* (1961).
(27) C.F. Palmstierna, *My Dearest Louise: Marie-Louise and Napoleon, 1813-1814* (1958).
(28) J.M. Thompson, *Napoleon's Letters* (Oxford, 1934).